D0885198

REPENTANCE-
the Joy-filled Life

M. Basilea Schlink

Translated by
Harriet Corbin
with
Sigrid Langer

ZONDERVAN PUBLISHING HOUSE
Grand Rapids, Michigan

REPENTANCE — THE JOY-FILLED LIFE

Copyright © 1968 by Zondervan Publishing House,
Grand Rapids, Michigan

Second printing   1970
Third printing   February 1971
Fourth printing   November 1971

Library of Congress Catalog Card Number: 68-56090

Printed in the United States of America

The author of this book may be contacted
at the following address:
    Canaan in the Desert
    9849 North 40th Street
    Phoenix, Arizona 85028

Contents

Chapter 1

A Confession

This book is really a confession of my own spiritual experiences. My Christian life began with a time of remorse and repentance. Later on I discovered the great joy of the life-renewing process of daily repentance.

A letter I wrote to my friend and fellow worker in 1936 tells how this came about. It was her birthday, and the scripture text on the calendar for that day read, "Who is a God like thee, pardoning iniquity!" (Micah 7:18) I wrote to her: "We can praise and glorify God for many things, but there is no rejoicing here on earth so great as the exultation over God's greatest gift: forgiveness of sins. This exultation, 'Praise the Lord, O my soul,' is heard not only here on earth but also in Heaven: 'There is joy over one sinner that repenteth.' And when one day all the songs and praises about the good things He has done for us in this life come to an end, another song will start in Heaven praising the Lamb who has taken away the sin of the world.

"Does this song of thanksgiving resound in our hearts, 'Who is a God like thee, pardoning iniquity,' or are our praises silent? If we are silent here, how can we sing in heaven at the throne of the Lamb when the saints there begin to sing His song? At the beginning of last year we did not know the joyful sound of this verse. When we first found Christ—you think of your confirmation classes and of the time in Kassel, and I think of my time in the Bible House—one of our favourite songs was— 'There is a fountain filled with blood drawn from

7

Immanuel's veins; and sinners plunged beneath that flood lose all their guilty stains . . .' But later, when I had to spend years studying and waiting, and you had to spend years practising your Social work, our hearts were so laden with the cares of this world that the song of the Lamb died out and our hearts no longer knew this joy of 'Who is a God like thee, pardoning iniquity!' We had adjusted ourselves to the fact that we were not victorious over our character weaknesses. We no longer suffered over our sinful nature, so it was no longer our daily experience that Jesus is our Deliverer. We could not, therefore, sing songs of rejoicing about our forgiveness and redemption. So without realizing it we continued along this path that led us farther and farther away from Christ.

"But God in His grace sought after us so that our hearts could once again sing the song of the Lamb, so that one day we might be at His side. Last year He forcibly brought us face to face with our sins and bondages—in our work this winter but especially last summer in regard to our relationship with X. That experience showed the both of us we cannot forgive, cannot be merciful, cannot suffer injustice, and cannot be good-tempered. If we stay the way we are, we will never be able to stand on the side of those who have overcome; and 'without holiness no one can see the Lord'. Oh, that God gave us this greatest gift during the last year—the recognition of our sin! Looking back on the lost years, no other verse could have been more appropriate for your birthday than this joyful shout of thanksgiving: 'Who is a God like Thee, pardoning iniquity!'

"Now we can begin our ministry. Previously, it would have been impossible. Without this shout of rejoicing in our hearts, how could we possibly carry the good news about the forgiveness of sins to others? We were lacking the power and authority for this ministry which we may only have if our hearts can rejoice and sing: 'His blood has carried all my sins away' (from a German hymn), and if we can point to the Lamb with sparkling eyes—the Lamb which has accomplished the greatest and most wonderful deed. Is not this a wonderful verse for this year? Seldom have we ever had such a verse. It does not only show us our sins which we experienced during the past year, but as the Word of God it is also a promise—a promise that this joyful shout: 'Who is a God like Thee, pardoning iniquity!' will resound in our hearts. Then our ministry will be blessed. With joy we will be able to testify to this gracious and merciful God who forgives us all our sins in Christ and who sets us free from the law of sin and death. The old year brought us the knowledge of our bondages and God's forgiveness. The new year, let us solemnly resolve, should bring us fervent battles and wrestling so we can overcome all our sins, 'whom the Son makes free will be free indeed.' We do not want to relax. We must be firm in our resolution to fight and pray for victory whatever the cost. We want to thank God for all the obstacles which He has placed in our way. Oh that we would learn to overcome them through continual loving! Oh that we would be the master of our sins! It is pure grace that God does not only reveal our sins, but that He also gives us the opportunity to learn how to be victorious and to overcome bit by bit. We must use the Word of God and every weapon He has given us, which will help us be victorious in this difficult battle with X. After being forgiven we want to attain His victory no matter what it costs. With thanksgiving we want to testify how God has helped us. We want to boast of His victory ..."

In the previous years I no longer cried over my sins. That is why I also did not know the joyful shout: "Who is a God like Thee ..." I could not bear a joyful witness to this God. The joy of heaven which should be our portion in Jesus was missing in my life.

9

Because my repentance at conversion did not continue as a daily experience, my love for Jesus grew lukewarm. Only penitent sinners—to whom forgiveness is given—are on fire with love for Jesus. So I can tell you that a life without daily repentance is spiritually poor. It has no joy or power and is totally lacking in fruit. Heaven is not "at hand" in such a life.

I can never thank God enough for showing me that this was the reason for my inner distress and the lack of victory in my struggle against sin. Here lay the cause for my spiritual death. The Lord showed me in a very practical way: He allowed my relationship to those with whom I was living to be utterly shipwrecked. He showed me I was unable to really love the ones who were hard to love. So He convicted me of my sins and gave me a contrite heart.

As I experienced renewed life and joy resulting from this repentance, it became my earnest prayer to receive this precious gift daily. Soon my fellow worker joined me in the same prayer for the young women we were leading in our Bible classes that they too would experience this awakening. God answered our prayers by working in their hearts as we studied together the teaching of His Word. Then in September 1944 God allowed us to be dealt a terrible blow in the bombing of our city of Darmstadt bringing death and destruction to thousands of people and homes. As a result of this holocaust, the young women in our classes underwent deep experiences of contrition and repentance and became keenly aware of the sins in their lives. Dead hearts were revived. These young women who lived through this time could testify with us of the tremendous grace they experienced.

Following the bombing the people of the city were filled with terror. We were under continuous attacks from low-flying aircraft strafing the city. The German army was defeated; the allies entered the city. But we who had gone to the depth of sorrow for our sins and turned from them in true repentance were finding Heaven amidst the destruction. This was especially true at a retreat we held with these young women. It lasted for several days amidst the roar of the military forces. I can truly tell you that joy was on the girls' faces because love and adoration for Jesus was in their hearts. The distress of war vanished in the reality of Heaven which was there. The word of John the Baptist had come true. "Repent, for the Kingdom of Heaven is at hand."

Our Sisterhood of Mary was born of that experience. It was formed by these same young women who attended our classes and who were together with my fellow worker and me in our retreat after the bombing. Later on, as the Sisterhood grew and developed, we in it learned repentance in the same way as in that terrible night's destruction. God disciplined us many times. We often found ourselves under His judgment. But He always waited patiently for us to respond to Him with broken and contrite hearts so that He could again give Heaven to us and Himself in it.

... Often He waited long for his answer! But mercifully God's Spirit did not allow us peace until He had again brought us anew to contrition and repentance.

In our Sisterhood we have a certain time of "walking in the light" together. These times are our greatest help in bringing us into repentance. In these times we are revealed in His light—confessing and acknowledging our guilt before God and each other. We experience again and again the results of our "Fellowships in the Light"—repentance, joy and renewed life! The songs of praise and great rejoicing in our festivals and celebrations come from this practice. Yes, this joy permeates our entire life.

Therefore, praise and adoration to God, the Holy Spirit who awakens in hard, dead men the grace of repentance. He gives it to those who ask for it. In this way "the Kingdom of Heaven is at hand".

Chapter 2

Repentance—
A Creative, Life-giving Power

Long ago John the Baptist cried out, "Repent, the Kingdom of Heaven is at hand." Is that not the very basis of the Gospel, the Good News? Repentance—the gate to heaven! Repentance—the gate to the very heart of the Father! Yes, repentance makes us joyful and blissful. It brings us home to the heart of the Father; it brings us all the way to heaven. It is a gift of the Holy Spirit, who inclines Himself to a human heart, which is hard and brittle. He breaks it into small pieces, so that the Father, the Creator God, can take these pieces into His hand and create a new vessel for His honour.

Should we not long for this gift more than all others? It is a piece of divine life, of true life. Only when a heart can cry and rejoice is it alive. Only a dead person no longer stirs. He is stiff. He can no longer move. He is unable to feel joy or happiness, even unable to weep. However, a person who lives in repentance has the characteristics of life. He cries. He cries over the one thing that is worth crying over, because it contains our ruin and the ruin of all men, because it brings death and terrible judgment and horrible consequences here and in all eternity—he cries over sin. Greatly sorrowed by his sin, he no longer cries over things which are not worthy to be cried over—compared with this sorrow, they are only a trifle, a transient matter. One who gets too disturbed over temporal things falls into a sadness that leads to death (II Corinthians 7:10). However, through repentance we only cry over things which have such terrible consequences; through repentance we have the true godly grief.

Those who are repentant are realists. They are grieved over their sins at the right time; others, who neglect to do this, will be sorry for their sins for all eternity. They are grieved over their sins now so that they can turn over a new leaf and begin to lead a new and different life.

Yes, those who repent are truly alive, for after weeping over their sins they break out in rejoicing which is unknown to other hearts. The joy of forgiveness—no other joy can compare in depth and height! The joy of redemption—no other happiness could ever compare! A person who has been imprisoned in chains rejoices when he is freed. And yet his imprisonment was only for a number of years, and his freedom is also limited by time. However, here it is a matter of being imprisoned by the Prince of this world and of the regions of hell, an imprisonment which would have lasted for all eternity and from which no man could have freed them. And now the release has come from a different side. He came down from heaven, became man, let Himself be taken prisoner and condemned to death—in our stead so that we could go free. Shouldn't that fill our souls with rejoicing beyond anything we have ever known? Only contrition and repentance let us partake of this joy-filled life. They let us sense our imprisonment and our death. They drive us into the arms of our Redeemer, our life-giving Lord.

Therefore, people who have not yet experienced repentance, even though they are pious and faithful churchgoers, are spiritually dead. This is what our Lord said in His letter to the church at Sardis: "You have the name of being alive, and you are dead" (Revelation 3:1). To live means to repent. Dead are those Christians who have never wept over their sins or who have long ago ceased to weep over their sins. Dead are those Christians—in God's eyes—who no longer rejoice and sing, because God has forgiven them their sins. Wherever this joy is missing, even though we call ourselves believing and faithful Christians, there is something wrong in our lives. For just as it is true that we continually sin and continually need forgiveness, it is also true that repentance must continually pour into our hearts.

Yes, contrition and repentance must become the very basis of our life. Otherwise, our whole Christianity is on the downward path and we will become like the "proudly exultant ones" of Zephaniah, who says that they will fall under severe judgment (Zephaniah 3:11).

Therefore, repentance must be the foundation of our life. A repentant attitude is the only proper attitude which we can have towards God. Can we come before a Holy God in any other position than lying on our faces before Him as broken sinners?—for we daily sin against Him. Furthermore, repentance must be our foundation of life, because we daily sin against our fellow men. Truly, there is no one among us who lives completely in love. For that reason we must lie with broken hearts before the difficult ones with whom we live and work, those we often sin against by not helping in love to find the right path.

"Repent!" That is the call of Scripture. Time and again Jesus calls us to repent. And it was the call of Martin Luther. He fought against lifeless and false Christianity, against the self-assurance and pride, with which we dare to approach God and which causes the divine life in us to die. Do we realize how much the Lord Jesus is interested in our living in this repentant attitude so that by it we may have abundant access to eternal life? Otherwise the unrepentant attitude of the early Church would not have caused Him to pronounce such a harsh verdict: 'You say I am rich, I have prospered, and I need nothing; not knowing, that you are wretched, pitiable, poor, blind and naked. So because you are lukewarm and neither cold nor hot, I will spew you out of my mouth" (Revelation 3:16, 17).

Isn't this also true today? If I think I am in the right in all my human relationships, that I have done all that is necessary to repair the hard feelings I have caused, then I have a complacent attitude which is exactly the opposite of the repentant attitude. Then I declare that Life, Jesus Himself, who would come to me in repentance, has no room in my heart. To the complacent and self-satisfied Jesus says in His letters to the seven churches: "Repent!" Yes, He begs us: Turn away from this attitude which brings destruction to the believers. Only those who overcome will remain in the Book of Life (Revelation 3:2–5). It is only repentance that saves us from death and leads us to eternal life and allows us to experience a foretaste of that life now.

Only those who are alive can bring life to others. Dead people are unable to reproduce life by word or deed. They are simply dead. Whoever does not live in repentance belongs to the spiritually dead, who cannot bring anyone to life. But the repentant one is full of life, full of divine life and able therefore, to beget it in others. Whenever someone repents, he scarcely needs to say a word. He doesn't need to preach to others. Rather, when he lies prostrate before God and man and confesses with a broken and contrite heart: "I have sinned. I am guilty," his words have the power of life. They open the hardest hearts and bring life to the dead. These words spoken by the prodigal son, as he lay weeping before his father, caused the father's heart to overflow with love. The same thing happens whenever we confess our sin and admit our guilt before men. When we ask them for forgiveness, their hearts are opened. Tears of contrition soften the hardest, most unforgiving hearts—even though some cases may take longer than others. Tears of contrition transform us and others. They give birth to love and new life.

What a creative, life-giving power is inherent in repentance! For that reason our Lord Jesus, and Peter, too, on the day of Pentecost, commanded the churches of His faithful followers, "Repent." This is the way to be brought to life and filled with the Holy Spirit, for it is in repentance that the Kingdom of Heaven is at hand.

Chapter 3

Repentance Brings the Kingdom of Heaven Down to Earth

"Repent, for the Kingdom of Heaven is at hand." Isn't that what we are all longing for? Don't we all wish that a bit of the Kingdom of Heaven would come and be formed among us? Kingdom of Heaven! That means joy and peace. That means that love reigns. That means that there is true joy, because Jesus is really in our midst.

But where can we find such a church or Christian group which depicts the Kingdom of Heaven? The people who work together would have to live in love and complete unity. The spirit of adoration would have to be alive. Joy would have to shine on all the faces. Yes, places that radiate Heaven attract people—even those who no longer want to have anything to do with the Church. Everyone would like to experience something of Heaven upon this poor earth, because everyone, even the most irreligious person, hungers for joy, love and peace. Everyone hungers for a bit of Heaven. The word "Heaven" strikes a note in every human heart, for all men are Adam's children, driven out of paradise but still longing for what they have lost. When they find a portion of that lost paradise, a little bit of Heaven on earth, they are attracted to it. There they will learn to believe in Jesus again—Jesus who is the Lord of the Kingdom of Heaven, He who alone represents the very nature of Heaven itself—peace, love and joy—everything that man longs for.

How distressing that we Christians in our various

churches, groups, brotherhoods and sisterhoods represent that Kingdom so poorly, even though our Lord Jesus said that He had brought the Kingdom of Heaven to us! How tragic that our sermons about the love and glory of Jesus Christ convince so few people. We preach about love but do not show it; we talk about God's goodness but do not demonstrate it. They cannot find any place where they can go to see a bit of the Kingdom of Heaven and see how good the Lord is! Jesus, however, only came to build the Kingdom of Heaven. At the start of His ministry He said that the Kingdom of Heaven was dawning. Now He is waiting for it to be established among us. He went the bitter way to death not only to open the door to Heaven above for us, but also to redeem us here on earth. And wherever the redeemed are together, there is a bit of the Kingdom of Heaven. They depict it as men in whom love, peace, joy, reconciliation, kindness and gentleness live. Where these fruits exist we truly experience a foretaste of Heaven.

Yes, both God and the world are waiting and crying for the manifestation of the Kingdom of Heaven among Christians. When God says, "The Kingdom of Heaven is at hand," should it not be seen somewhere? In the Person of Jesus it drew near to us, it was offered to us. That was the reason why He came. He brought Heaven down to earth. Wherever Jesus, the Lord of Heaven appeared, a bit of Heaven also appeared on earth. Those who were with Him tasted it. They tasted the love of the Father. They tasted the goodness, compassion and loving care of God. Those who were with Him tasted the forgiveness of the Father. They tasted the love which healed all the wounds of their souls. They tasted the joy and exultation that all sinners receive who come to the Saviour. Those who could see Jesus and hear the blessed words from His mouth and could experience His love were filled with joy and jubilation.

When Jesus Christ, the Head, ascended to Heaven, His body the church remained here. And this body is now to bring the Kingdom of Heaven to men. When they come into contact with His Members, they should be healed in body and soul. They should also rejoice, be comforted and be healed of their wounds. They should also wherever they come together with members of His body experience compassion, forgiveness, and forbearing love, a true foretaste of Heaven.

"The Kingdom of Heaven is at hand" is what Jesus could say when He came to earth. He says the same thing now about His church. However, let us ask ourselves, "Where is it at hand?" Is it possible to say: "Go to this house or this church and there you will become happy, there you will be healed of the sufferings of your soul, there you will be surrounded with love so much that it will seem as if you are born anew. You will taste the fullness of joy because eternal joy is there." Is not the opposite true? That is why there is no attraction for those who do not know Jesus. No wonder the masses of men, God's creatures, prefer to go to the woods and parks on Sunday. There in the midst of the creation of God they experience something of the joy and beauty which nature reflects. This gives them a bit of the joy that every human heart longs for. When they go to church, they often do not sense any joy, they do not see it on the faces, they do not find the radiance of God in the churches as they do out in nature. Where do they hear joyful singing in the churches? Where do they sense that the hearts are really singing along, so that their hearts will also be swept along to joy in their Lord Jesus Christ?

Where are the child-like and trusting people in the church who reveal the truth of Jesus' saying: the Kingdom of Heaven belongs to those who become like little children, and because they are like little children

20

they will experience that Kingdom now? (Matthew 18:3). Yes, where are the child-like souls in God's church who have the power to attract unbelievers who then in the light of this child-like joy too might find Heaven's joy?

To a great extent Christianity today is lived mostly in the realm of reason: so stiff, so unchildlike and therefore so joyless. This grieves the heart of God that His churches are so lacking in simplicity and child-likeness, that they actually radiate less of the Kingdom of Heaven that His creation does. They do not reflect His Kingdom so have no attraction for those who do not know Him.

Do we have any idea how much God suffers because of what we continually do to Him? Or, expressed in human words, which the Holy Scriptures use again and again in order to show us the heart of God: How disappointed God is in us! He is especially disappointed by those who belong to Him. They don't depict Him. And they are the ones whom He has bought and redeemed with the blood of His Son. They are to be His real witnesses. They are to bring others to Him. How painful it is for God! The stones, all of nature must preach because we His church keep silence. We do not radiate the joy of redemption and are such poor witnesses for Him.

Now comes the great question: Why is there so little of God's Kingdom in our midst that the world does not recover, that people are not attracted, that souls and bodies are not healed, that the sad are not comforted? Why? There is one word which brings in the Kingdom of Heaven: "Repent!" It is a call as mighty as a peal of thunder. It is a call which cannot be ignored. It is so loud and clear. It is a call which concerns us sinners. Yes, it is not simply *a* call; it is *the* call of Scripture. Whoever does not heed this call, will not receive any gift or blessing from

God—not even forgiveness. It is a holy law of Scripture, that God with His blessings, His Kingdom only comes down to a humble soul, that is, to a sinner who has repented. The Kingdom of Heaven remains closed to all others. The Kingdom of God, the Kingdom of Heaven, is a Kingdom full of grace and only he who lies prostrate at the feet of Jesus in contrition and repentance will be blessed.

The first characteristic of the Kingdom of Heaven—joy, great joy—will be kindled through contrition and repentance. Repentance is the only gate through which the Gospel is received. Repentance is the entrance to the joy-filled life with Christ. It is the prerequisite for attaining forgiveness, and wherever forgiveness is received there is salvation and joy. Contrition and repentance contain great bliss; they bring the grace of forgiveness to those who were actually damned for time and eternity. Contrition and repentance bring us joy, because they move God to reaccept us as His children: "Your sins are forgiven you." Yes, repentance brings the joy of Heaven. When a contrite, repentant son returns home, the Father not only takes him in His arms and embraces him, but He also clothes him in His garment of righteousness. He puts on him a ring of love and the most beautiful jewels which will one day shine in Heaven. The repentant are rich. They who no longer have any right to demand anything from God and man, who are the very poorest creatures become rich in grace and gifts. They lie before God and men acknowledging their guilt as the most miserable sinners. All they can do is wait for God to look upon them with favour, to wait for a gift, the gift of forgiveness which is pronounced over them.

What gives more joy than the word of amnesty spoken to a condemned man? It makes him sing and dance with joy! In this way the Kingdom of Heaven draws near—it is "at hand". Yes, the Kingdom of Heaven, the Kingdom where everyone rejoices and sings, dawns in a heart which has received forgiveness.

The Kingdom of Heaven is also the kingdom of love. But we are only able to love when He first loves us, and He loves the contrite heart of the penitent sinner. Jesus did not come for the righteous, but for sinners. He bestows His gifts of love and forgiveness on those who come to Him, the Saviour, filled with remorse and repentance. In this love which tasted death for them and pronounced forgiveness upon the cross, they will become whole. Such broken hearts have only one desire: to love the One who has loved them so much. They are so overwhelmed that He bore their sins and carried them away. When we receive forgiveness, our hearts become so filled with rejoicing that we cannot help but to love Him with a boundless love. We cannot help but give our lives to Him who gave His life for us and saved us from sin's prison. We cannot cease thanking Him and serving Him with all our talents and strength. This is the essence of Heaven—everything centres around Jesus, everyone loves Him above all else.

Repentance gives us a taste of the Kingdom of Heaven and all its blessings because it brings wonderful, overflowing love. The greatest longing of a Christian is to love Jesus. How many people sigh, "If I could love Jesus with all my heart, life would have meaning and satisfaction. I would be the person He wants me to be, able to respond to His love. Life would then be rich, and I would be happy!'

What a joyful message we have that repentance is the way that leads us to overflowing and wholehearted love for Jesus, bringing with it such a great treasure of grace and mercy. We see this in the case of Mary Magdalene. She brought nothing but her sin to Jesus, and what a terrible sin it was. But her life was changed as she stood

23

before Him with repentant heart receiving His forgiveness. She was enriched and transformed by His great love. What an example she is for us! Yes, God's command: "Repent!" is truly the gate through which we enter the kingdom of love, the Kingdom of Heaven. There is no other gate, no other way to enter it or through which it can come to us.

But is it not true that every one who has confessed Jesus Christ as Saviour once fell down at the foot of the cross as a repentant sinner, received forgiveness, and in this way entered the Kingdom of God? And yet how can it be that His Kingdom is not formed in the churches or communities in which they live? How many times the Scripture teaches by word and example that we may lose the grace we have received. No one has obtained a guaranteed entrance to the Kingdom of God by being converted or baptized. It is always possible to lose this privilege. Remember the unforgiving servant! When one does not forgive his brother, and has bitterness in his heart and no compassion for others, he loses the grace he has received. Who among us does not experience this time and again? There is only one way to receive God's grace and continually experience the Kingdom of Heaven: We must take refuge in the cross; we must come immediately to our Lord, and when necessary to men, in contrition and repentance. Thus, we prepare the way for the Kingdom of Heaven.

Wherever we repent with contrite hearts, Jesus Christ will draw near. He will come into our midst and bring the Kingdom of Heaven with Him, which is always there where He is. The thief on the cross confessed: "We are receiving the just rewards of our deeds" (Luke 23:41). He asked Jesus for mercy and Jesus responded by promising him that very day he would be with Him in paradise. This blessed experience of the thief should become ours also. As we come before Him with repentant hearts, He gives paradise to us on earth that we may live with Him now in this life. Truly, the Kingdom of Heaven is at hand where sinners repent.

Chapter 4

Repentance: God's Call to the Church for the Salvation of the People

"Repent!" Who among us hears His call? Jesus is going now to Christian churches throughout the world knocking at the hearts of individuals with a loud voice, expecting some to hear Him. This call is first given to the church, rather than to unbelievers, because judgment must begin in God's house. But the question is: do we listen to God's voice, to His judgments and His punishments, for if we listen would we not experience life-renewing change? When God is judging us, His family, He is waiting for the answer, our repentance. The first concern today is not for those who are far away from God—as much as we should pray for them—but for those who know Him in the church, that they repent.

Surely there is great need for repentance in the church, for down in the very depth of our beings we have hardened our hearts against God's Spirit. Jesus' last commandment to love one another has been answered with hatred, division, and judging of one another. Though the Ecumenical Council has brought a new relationship among the denominations, how much judging, criticizing, contending and disputing still goes on. We do not treat each other as brothers in Christ. Walls of doctrine still exist among our various Christian churches while our enemy Satan has his armies lined up and ready for the final battle. Many groups and factions already are united on the anti-Christian front.

In our day, the greatest need among true Christians is

for unity, that we may be strong, able to resist the attacks of the enemy. The only way for God's people to be united in love—as Jesus prayed that they would be as a sign to the world—is the pathway of remorse and repentance. The great sorrow of disunity will never be ended until every Christian within every group and denomination begins to repent, even while he is still being criticized by those who oppose him. Each one of us must daily come to Jesus, and bow down before His cross with our guilt, because we, the limbs of His body, are envious of each other, still quarrelling and fighting, sinning against Jesus Himself.

But most of all, the church has grieved the heart of God by declaring in certain places that God is dead. We all share in this blasphemy by demonstrating with our lives a dead rather than a living God. We must realize that the "God is dead" theology sweeping the world, is not caused by the intellectual problem that modern man, within the context of his mind, is unable to accept God. But rather it is proclaimed today because we in Christendom are dead—"dead in sin". And because we are unwilling to face our sins and failures we proclaim God "dead" with our lives, perhaps without knowing it. When we no longer see ourselves as sinners needing to repent before a holy God, we no longer need a living Saviour and lose our very concept of a living, Holy God. God's commandments, the holy declaration of His will, are declared dead in most of His churches and no longer binding to His children. So we affix the seal of death with theological argument and pronounce in book and pulpit, "God is dead."

Instead of rebelling against this doctrine we adjust ourselves to the spirit of the age: our lives change to agree with the ideas and needs of modern man with his ethics and moral practices. Who among us in the church repents for all this blasphemy and disobedience towards God? The spirit of contrition and repentance is unknown to most of us for it means that we must turn back to God and His commandments instead of making God conform to our demands. There is little power even in our evangelistic meetings and crusades because tears of contrition are not shed. God's church no longer wants to recognize or hear about His laws. What dishonour this brings to Him!

We do not see that the signs of the times, for which Jesus told us to watch, have been fulfilled when God is declared dead and the infallibility of His authority denied even in the church. We do not see that we help to bring about the darkness of the last days by apathetically accepting and adjusting ourselves to this attitude. The increasing lawlessness and the cooling of our love—what Jesus called signs of the end time—seem harmless in the church, though examples may be seen as never before. Think of the great increase of crime in the last few years, of the glorification of brutality and sexual perversion. Think of the various kinds of addiction that have gripped millions, of the tremendous increase in practice of occultism and spiritism, the satanic cults.

All these things are prevalent even among Christian people. It is happening in the very midst of the church communities. Are not these signs a call to fast and pray, to turn about and be converted? It was prophesied to the pagan city of Nineveh that they would be destroyed. But they repented, so God saved them. How much more should repentance start in our modern day church with fasting and prayer, that God's mighty judgment does not fall on us in proportion to our blasphemy and sacrilege. Because of our love for Jesus, who pities mankind and His church's devastation; because of our love for men ("save some by snatching them out of the fire", Jude 23), the word of Joel 2:15 must be heard today: "Blow the trumpet in Zion; sanctify a fast; call a solemn assembly." It no longer can be done by traditional prayer. It must now be praying that has become weeping, crying: Lord spare your people! Do not allow them—the church of your New Testament—to honour false Gods, to deny and dishonour you so that the unbelievers laugh and say, "Now where is your God?" In days of old the Lord's people wept and prayed and . . . "God repented of the evil which he had said he would do to them, and he did not do it" (Jonah 3:10). Do not make God wait for our prayers and supplication. He wants to act according to His Word: "Now therefore amend your ways and your doings, and obey the voice of the Lord your God, and the Lord will repent the evil which He has pronounced against you" (Jeremiah 26:13).

God's church today must hear this call. It is the very foundation of God's Kingdom upon which everything is built: the mercy that is offered to us individually and as God's people. It is the firm basis on which our spiritual house must be founded so that when stormy weather comes it is not washed away. Only that which is built on the firm foundation of contrition and repentance will last for eternity, will bear real fruit for God. O that true repentance would be again the chief desire both for us as individuals and for our churches! For it results in God's mercy flowing towards us producing His salvation.

Chapter 5

The Way to Repentance

Nothing is more important than finding the way to repentance—for with it comes great joy and a new life. The first step is for us to realize the fact that we do not have repentance. This is fundamental because there is nothing we lack more, since the fall of man, than this one thing. The prophets of the Old Testament were the first to speak of God's desire for the people to repent, then John the Baptist gave the call, and finally Jesus Himself: "Would that even today you knew the things that make for peace" (Luke 19:42).

Because of our human predisposition, we are apathetic and indifferent towards our sins, much of the time being unaware of them. We weep easily over the difficulties of our lives, over things that have been done to us: our sorrows, griefs, and disappointments. But because it is not natural to our human nature, few of us come to the place of real contrition and repentance. The heart of man has a way of thinking it is always in the right and sees no reason to weep over its own sins. Our human nature is self-righteous and impenitent. We want to blame others rather than ourselves. We even blame God and say His ways are incomprehensible to us.

The first step then is for us to realize we have no repentance. After seeing this, we are ready for the second step: to know we cannot generate it ourselves. No one is able to change his own hard heart into one that is soft and broken, able to weep over its own sins. This must be accomplished in us by a work of grace which is a gift of God.

We must look with faith towards omnipotent God rather than to ourselves, for we have a God who performs miracles, and that is our hope. We have a God who says: "Is anything impossible with me!" His good pleasure is to create, by His Holy Spirit, something in our hearts that was not there before. He is able—to His glory—to perform the miracle of melting the hardest hearts. When Jesus on the cross destroyed Satan's power He also destroyed the hardness of our hearts, the blindness towards our own sin with which the enemy had bound us. He destroyed our unrepentance and won for us the ability to weep over our sins. He made it possible for us to know tears of sorrow, not only for the suffering we have brought to God but also for the suffering we have brought to men. Jesus' call, "Repent", is not only a command, it is also a promise. For with every commandment God provides His power with which we can obey it. This was done for us at Golgotha in the sacrifice of Jesus who overcame in the crucifixion and resurrection all principalities and powers that could hinder us from true repentance.

When we continue faint-heartedly and excuse ourselves by saying that we were unable to have a penitent heart, it is a sign that our thinking has been clouded by the enemy. And because man likes to have an excuse for everything, we finally blame God and say that He has not given us this gift.

But we really have no excuse. Jesus obtained repentance for us on the cross. God shows us that we can experience it by the prayer of faith, trusting in Jesus' victory. When we recognize the hardness of our own hearts, our inability to repent in our own strength, we can then pray believing in Jesus' promise: "Everything you ask in my name will be given to you." Yes, we may pray this prayer for a penitent heart in Jesus' name because He came to free us from self-righteousness. He came that we might be repentant sinners returning home like the prodigal son. Whoever goes to God with this prayer, trusting in His help, will not be disappointed. For inherent within the promise is the certainty of being heard. When I daily ask: "Lord, give me the grace of repentance, give me a broken heart, enlighten my eyes that I may see the beam in them and realize my own sin against God and men," He will hear me. He will open my eyes so I can see the depth of my sins, the pain I have caused in others rather than what they have done to me. I will then see things in the light of God's truth rather than in the darkness of the enemy who puts the sins of others before me like a huge screen which blinds my eyes and blocks me from seeing my own sins.

The prayer for the light of God's truth to come into our hearts, our talking and acting, is important so we may be freed from the darkness in which the enemy has wrapped us. He wants to keep us from seeing the truth of our sinful nature. He does not want us to be repentant sinners whose lives are filled with holiness, joy and power. But we do not have to stay longer under the enemy's spell. Jesus says, "I am the light of the world; he who follows me, will not walk in darkness, but will have the light of life." His light is truth which casts its searchlight on our pathway, that we may see when we go astray.

It is still not enough to pray daily that God would give me the light of truth. It is still not enough to ask daily that the grace of repentance be given to me. For every day I must accept the Lord's chastening. I only show repentance when I daily pray: "Father, do with me whatever You must do; chasten me and break me into pieces so that afterwards You can give me a humble, penitent heart." More Christians have come to repentance through God's punishments than through sermons on the need for repentance. Those who long for the grace of repentance must pray for the willingness to accept God's punishments, that our hearts may become soft and broken. Repentance does not fall from Heaven like a rain of grace. It must be prayed for and received by faith. But it must also be received through chastening and suffering; and when we do not fear it, the walk on God's pathway of discipline is rewarding, for it bears the most wonderful fruit.

It is almost incomprehensible the way a holy life grows out of contrition and repentance! All true joy and happiness, all power in our work for God's kingdom depends on living in this grace, weeping day by day over our sins, continually bowing down before God and men. It is of the greatest importance that we continue praying, imploring for repentance to be given to us, never failing to watch for the obstacles which hinder us in receiving it. It is also of the greatest importance that we are willing to accept His way of punishment and discipline which will bring us to repentance and allow Christ to be formed in us.

> O Holy Ghost, I beg of Thee
> A penitent humility
> The greatest of Thy graces.
> For all my sins do Thou impart
> Abundant sorrow to my heart,
> To make me truly humble.

> O Holy Ghost, I beg of Thee
> To break my heart's obduracy,
> That it may start lamenting,
> Lamenting loud for all my sins,
> The cause of my dear Saviour's pains,
> Who bore my guilt away.

O Holy Ghost, I beg of Thee
That Thou my Advocate may be,
And plead my wordless longing.
Thou seest, hard as stone, my heart,
Compunction deep to me impart,
Help me to rue my sinning.

Spirit of Penitence, I pray,
Give me another heart today,
A broken heart, most humble;
Before both God and man to bow,
My sins no pride of heart allow,
Thy love so deeply grieving.

Thou art the One who shall impart,
A truly contrite, lowly heart,
As promised by our Saviour.
Show me my sins and humble me,
That I by grace may pardoned be,
Restored to loving favour.

(Translated by Deaconess Joan Bindon –
Auckland, New Zealand)

Chapter 6

The Main Obstacles in Coming to Repentance

PART I: *No Repentance, Because We Are Proud, Self-righteous and Unwilling*

The chief obstacle to repentance is our own self-righteousness. This is especially true of the Christian, for the danger of self-righteousness is greatest for him. It is truly a miracle when a pious person weeps tears of sorrow for his life and lives continuously in a state of repentance. Therefore, our first concern must be to recognize this ugly sin so Jesus can come to us as Saviour of sinners, whether it be an individual, a church, or a Christian community such as our Sisterhood.

Self-justification—claiming one's innocence, and in so doing often blaming God—is an inheritance from Adam. The worst criminals have this urge to exonerate themselves. They claim innocence in the face of the most heinous crimes. Prison chaplains write that there is no place like a prison to find so many self-righteous people who claim they are unjustly imprisoned. We human beings think we are always in the right. We see no need to change, no need to repent. We excuse ourselves and refuse to admit our guilt.

In defending ourselves, we often become angry and abusive to others. We think it is perfectly right to react in this way because we have not been shown respect, have not been treated properly. We cannot allow others to treat us like slaves. We must defend ourselves! It does not matter that we have been furious and abusive and have spoken angry words. Our feelings were hurt. Is it our fault if we are sensitive and easily upset? Even when someone commits adultery it is something he really didn't want to do. He was just unable to control himself when too greatly aroused. Is it his fault that God created him this way? How unfair to be made to suffer all his life for something that he really didn't want to do!

Or we have been misunderstood and mistreated in our marriage. Then God brought a person into our life who was created just for us, with whom we could have perfect harmony of heart and soul. Was it a sin when we became attached to this person? The worst did not even happen! Or we are filled with bitterness, envy and hatred because of our lack of success in life. Or we are always a wallflower unable to influence other people with our beauty or charm. Or we are not gifted, have no great intelligence. How can we be different when God has made us the way we are?

We can go on thinking in this way, unaware that we are blaming God. But in so doing, we refuse Jesus Himself admittance to our life. He, as Saviour and giver of happiness, would make our life joyful, peaceful and full of His light. Instead, we blame Him for giving us our bad dispositions, our unstable nerves, or our lack of ability. We blame Him for allowing us such severe punishment for our anger and bitterness, our little lies, or our adultery. These things happened because we had to defend ourselves, or when the urge of our human nature—which He created—was too strong. It is no different now than in the past: Jesus is the guilty one, and we blame Him rather than ourselves. It does not matter that we have sinned and destroyed the lives of others.

Because of these excuses—why we did this or that, or that we had to talk or act in this way for our own self-defence—we have grown blind. We do not see that sin is still sin and guilt is still guilt, and we are responsible for it.

It is apparent how self-righteous the heart is—accusing God rather than itself—in statements that are made time and again, even in Christian circles, about distress of war and other miseries in the world today. People say: "How can God allow it; how can He permit the evil on the earth that is caused by men?" Self-righteousness makes us so blind and deaf that we no longer recognize God's voice speaking to us through war and other distresses. We do not recognize that these judgments are His final wooing of us. We no longer see how He abundantly comforts those who come to Him amidst the judgments and bow willingly under His hand expecting help and comfort from Him alone; how He changes, by His presence, hell to heaven in prison camps and other terrible places. Self-righteousness makes us so blind that we do not see that man alone is entirely responsible for all the misery here on earth. We do not want to obey God. If we obeyed Him and lived according to His commandments, He would not have to judge and punish us, and heaven would be here on earth.

By remaining so self-righteous we grieve His heart to-day in the same way as His accusers did when He was on His way to His passion. When we claim that we or our country or mankind are not guilty, we are blaming God who above all else is a God of love. We are blaming Jesus who died for our sins, who is Saviour, Comforter and source of all joy. But He is Saviour only for those who want to be saved, who come to Him as sick, needy, miserable sinners. To His people today, just as He did when He was here on earth, He says, "Repent". He is waiting, in His boundless love, for those who will respond, so He can help them. It is unmistakably clear that we are guilty sinners for only sinners need to repent, to change their ways. When we honestly face this call, accepting it as truth, it must convict us.

"Repent" means "take stock of yourself, take account of yourself, look and see what is wrong with you, where you are guilty". Take account of how you are wronging your brother whom you have not forgiven, whom you did not respect more than yourself, whom you did not love with a love that endures all. Take account of how you sinned against the eighth commandment by carrying unfavourable tales about another, not even knowing if they were true. Take account of how much you have compromised with the world so that you no longer take the truth seriously. Take account if you are still on Jesus' way, the way of the cross, the way of self-sacrifice. Yes, take stock of yourself! That is the meaning of the word "repent" in the letter to the Laodiceans (Revelation 3). That is the trumpet call from the Lord to His church where self-righteousness and lukewarmness are reigning, where one soothes himself by a formal fulfilment of the commandments and lives by "cheap grace". And so excuses himself.

But Jesus declared war on all excuses. He puts them under His judgment—the most severe judgment with which He always condemned the self-righteous, the Pharisees in His time. They read the Scriptures and apparently took them very seriously. They prayed and lived strict, pious lives. But they were under our Lord's condemnation. The Kingdom of Heaven was locked for them though they too were offered God's grace. For Jesus came as Saviour for them as well as for everyone else. But they excluded themselves. They did not accept the preaching of repentance because they clung to their own self-righteousness. While others bowed down before the call of John the Baptist to repent, they rejected it. They thought the message exaggerated and unnecessary for such as they. Perhaps they said to themselves, as many do today, that it is unhealthy, soul-searching introspection. But God is speaking, and our joy is in surrendering to His call. Responding with mental assent will not open Heaven to us. It will be opened only as we lie before Him with broken hearts coming this way again and again to the foot of the cross.

Our arguments—either theological or psychological—have one root: it is pride that causes us to reject repentance. For repenting means to humble oneself before God and men, changing our ways, making things right. With repentance one confesses: my former way was wrong—and that is humbling. No other sin is so persistent in our hearts—especially among Christians who believe in Jesus as Saviour—as the sin of pride. When it is said to us that we are slow or too fast, or too impetuous, something in our proud heart defends itself immediately. One works slowly because one is so thorough. One is hasty because one is so intense. One is impetuous because one has to tell something that is very important. How quickly one rejects the judgment of others. How quickly one blames the other person. We say, "He always finds fault with us. He is so critical. We can never do anything right. He does not understand us.' When one will not listen to the genuine complaints of other people, it is because of pride. A humble person is willing to listen to reason. He has the courage to hear the truth and to admit: "Yes, that is the truth. In this way I must change. I must turn around and be converted."

Jesus calls this attitude of excusing ourselves, of minimizing our own guilt and accusing others of blaming us unjustly, "seeing the beam in my brother's eye and the splinter in my own". Man, in his pride, excuses himself constantly. And because he does not blame himself and come to repentance, he does not change. The sin he does not admit blocks his way to Jesus. It is the unacknowledged, unrepented sin that separates us from

God and our fellow men, and causes us to come under judgment.

Oh, that we would listen to the voice of man—as he rebukes us in both small and large things—as the voice of God calling us to repentance. How else shall we hear than through God's agents, the ones who are placed beside us, who see and know our behaviour? We will have little experience of daily contrition and repentance if we do not listen to those who reprimand us, if we do not accept it as the voice of God. If we take seriously our confession that we are sinners who daily sin and daily need to come to repentance, we must listen to those who criticize us. For when remorse is lacking, our life is full of hypocrisy, and something vital is missing.

If I believe in the teaching "always sinners", daily repentance belongs with it, but not as a legalistic system of confession that follows a pattern. For on one day I will be more convicted of sin than on another day when I am experiencing the love and joy of His forgiveness. But it must be a continuing experience always resulting in the joy of a renewed life.

Therefore, in believers repentance must take precedence over self-righteousness and excuses. We must begin to admit the things with which our fellow men reproach us. When our conscience softly speaks, we must listen rather than silencing it with our excuses. We must declare war on all self-righteousness and excuses because they lead us—as the Lord Jesus always said in the gospels—straight to hell. We must start repenting over every word of excuse, over the smallest thought of excuse. We must take stock of ourselves, change, and turn away from such action.

Because of His fulfilled redemption on the cross which can free us from the spirit of self-righteousness, the Lord will hear our prayer and answer it. He will give us, again and again, broken hearts to which the Kingdom of

Heaven is open. Then we will be filled with His life, His love, and His joy.

PART 2: *No Repentance Because We Do Not Realize the Voice of God in His Judgments*

Why is it so difficult for Christian people to come into the way of repentance? One reason, in addition to our self-righteousness, is that we no longer see that all the distressing things that happen to us are in God's will for our lives. It is God's way of speaking to us. Because we do not see Him as a living God, we do not see that "no hair falls from our heads without His will". The smallest event in our life is directly within His will.

The Scripture tells us that it is specifically for our sanctification when God intervenes in our life through distress and sorrow (Hebrews 12:10). He chastens us to cleanse us from our faults that we may be purified. The hand of God is behind every sorrow we experience, and is for the purpose of leading us—because of His love—into the right path. When something must be changed in us, He speaks through chastening. He takes someone from us and leads us into loneliness; perhaps we have bound ourselves too much to the love of one person when He wants to be the centre of our love. Or He allows us to have sickness so we will draw closer to Him, will come to the place of repentance, will surrender our life to Him—or perhaps that we may learn more patience.

It does not matter, when the Lord works on our sinful nature, whether His chastening is for our punishment or for our purification. He wants to educate us—as an earthly father would—for the purpose of changing us into His image. This is what He is working towards during our entire life. The Apostle Paul, in Romans 8, says that we are called and redeemed so that we may be conformed to the image of Christ. This is why Jesus came to earth and went the way of death: to make it possible for us to share God's nature, to make it again possible to receive the image and likeness of God that was lost at Adam's fall. We must admit when He chastens us—if we are truly honest—that we still do not show forth His image. He will show us—if we ask Him—where we fall short. Then He will wait for us to repent of the fact that we, His children, reflect so poorly the image of our Father. This failure grieves Him and troubles our fellow men.

Oh, that it would penetrate our hearts how much He longs for our repentance so He might mould us and fill us with His light. When we resist Him by not repenting, by not walking in His way of suffering—perhaps even blaming God for leading us in such difficult paths—we block our own way to His grace, to being superabundantly blessed, to being transformed into His likeness.

God does not punish us for His pleasure but to achieve His purpose in us. How difficult we make it by resisting Him, by not being willing to bow down before Him. Instead we ask, "What did I do to deserve this?" We pity ourselves and feel like martyrs, especially when other people are the cause of our suffering. And because we are innocent, we feel we suffered unjustly and become sad and depressed. We are unwilling to bow down under the suffering that is caused by the people who make our lives difficult, so bitterness and self-pity come into our hearts. We dig ourselves deeper and deeper into martyrdom and become more and more depressed and unhappy and so we are caught in our own misery. We do not understand the reason why God must then lead us into even greater distress and suffering.

Sometimes more pious ones stop blaming God and say: "It is God's will." The Moslems also say, "It is the will of Allah," without knowing that God is a Father who educates His children. He disciplines them, as an earthly father would, so that they will repent. The father wants the child to change his ways.

A distressing thing exists among Christians: we do not recognize the Fatherhood of God, nor do we see the personal work of His hand in our discipline. We have lost the ability to hear His voice in our chastening, nor do we know that He is waiting for our repentance.

Because of this, we do not come to the place of repentance in our daily lives—where God wants us to have it. We only experience repentance when we have sinned seriously. But pious people seldom sin seriously—or so we think! We really do not take our worst sin seriously: that we judge and condemn others and think ourselves superior. We do not even feel the urge to repent of this sin. Punishment should help us take our sins more seriously before a Holy God—especially those we make appear so harmless. Holy Scripture teaches that there is a relationship between our sin and God's punishment—for God's holiness stands on His law and so also does His Father heart. And His laws cannot be broken without penalties being paid.

In our Sisterhood we have often experienced how things that happened to us in our daily lives—especially at the time we were building our Mother house and chapel—were related to our guilt. During the construction the sisters had to push a loader that was heavily loaded with sand. It was very hard to handle. We were always afraid that if it jumped the track we could not get it back on again, because most of the sisters did not have the strength to do it. One day it jumped the track six times. Could that be an accident when even a sparrow does not fall to the ground except by God's will? Should not every happening have something to tell us? Should not every distress—and that really was a distress in our workday life—be a word from God, a loving Father God who cares about everything and wants to speak to us through everything? The sister in charge called the others into the prayer tent where they asked God to show them the reason why their work was in vain. The sisters then confessed that that very morning they had judging thoughts in their hearts against each other. This was causing them to work badly together and resulted in throwing the loader off balance. The sisters then repented and were reconciled to each other—and truly, the loader did not jump the track again!

This story is important though it seems to deal with an inconsequential thing. But our life consists of such inconsequential things, and we should see in them God's call to repentance. I think of other things that happened during the time that we were constructing our buildings with our own hands. At first, we did not want to see the relationship between the things that happened and the hand of God. There was a long period of torrential rain. We finally clearly saw the relationship between this and our sin, and when we obeyed God's call to repentance, we experienced His grace, and the rain ceased. It was the same way in times of severe frost or very hot weather when God gave them as hindrances to the construction of the buildings. Proud modern man has put himself above the Word of God and does not see His hand in all the events of his life both great and small. We read in the Scripture of the relationship between the weather and God's dealing with men: Leviticus 26:4; Deuteronomy 11:14; 28:12; I Kings 17:1. In Amos 4:7, we see where God spoke personally to one man through the elements: "And I also withheld the rain from you when there were yet three months to the harvest; I would send rain upon one city and send no rain upon another city; one field on which it did not rain withered."

When God moves heaven and earth to bring us to remorse and repentance, should not we be willing to hear

His voice and respond to it? Oh, that we would use all the events of our lives—especially the sorrowful ones—to receive the grace of repentance and give God the answer for which He longs. How precious is a tear of remorse to Him! Truly, it means more to Him than a hundred "good deeds". There is joy in Heaven over one soul that lies with broken heart before God. When the angels are filled with joy over such souls, how much more is the heart of Jesus! How God inclines His love to the repentant ones and draws them to His heart! These are the ones with whom He can do great deeds. For He builds His glory on our nothingness through which He can shine. He reveals Himself through the broken ones rather than the arrogant and proud, who, unaware of their own sins, sit in judgment on others.

Our repentance will not only bring joy to God's heart—by accomplishing that for which He sent the punishment—but also will bring joy to us. It will help us to grow into His image. When we listen immediately to His voice, future punishment will be spared us, and we can then more easily be led on the way of sorrow that Jesus has walked. Then we as priests can suffer for others "that they also may obtain salvation", as the Apostle Paul has written (II Timothy 2:10).

For our priestly suffering, of which the Scripture often speaks, there is no possible starting place other than repentance. When I suffer for another sinner and his guilt, I can do it only when I suffer first for my own sins and guilt. Only one person suffered for others being Himself innocent and pure, and that was Jesus Christ. He alone was the perfect sacrifice for sin. We can only suffer with Him as the limbs of His body; and when, through suffering, we are placed in the earth as grains of wheat to die, He will bring forth the fruit. This is true because He died for us sinners that we too might give our lives for the brethren (I John 3:16).

Self-righteousness, pride and resistance to God's punisments block our repentance. But there is something else than hinders us. It is the question: By what yardstick do I measure my life? If I am content with the standard: I have not murdered or robbed, I go to church, I pray, I keep the holy days, it will be unlikely that I will receive the gift of repentance. But our Lord tells us, "Unless your righteousness exceeds that of the Scribes and Pharisees (they kept the commandments and led good pious lives), you will never enter the Kingdom of Heaven" (Matthew 5:20).

Our Lord Jesus had a different standard of measurement from ours. He said that one who is angry with his brother will fall under judgment; that we are to leave our gift at the altar only after we have been reconciled to our brother. This is not only when we have been the offender, but even if another has offended us—if there is any bad feeling between us regardless of whose fault it is.

What a high standard Jesus sets for us: loving our enemies! Who comes up to this? Most of us come in contact with people in the family, at work, or in the neighbourhood who give us trouble and distress, who treat us badly; yes, who even perhaps torment us. How do we respond? Do we show them the love we are to have for enemies, or do we have bitter, judging thoughts and talk against them? Jesus calls this sin and says it will cause us to fall under judgment. And His Word is truth. He says, "Till heaven and earth pass away, not an iota, not a dot will pass from the law" (Matthew 5:18). The Sermon on the Mount is Jesus' law, the law of love which is the law of God's Kingdom.

One will always appear guilty when measured with

God's yardstick, instead of his own, and so will come easily to the place of contrition and repentance. By God's yardstick I am revealed as a guilty sinner in relationship to my brother who has something against me. I have sinned against the law of love because I did not treat him with merciful, humble, upholding love. So I have cause for sorrow and should come easily to repentance. If I do not seek God's standard of measurement I will not find the gateway to repentance, which is God's way to new life. Love stems from it, superabundant love toward Jesus and superabundant love toward men, even the hostile ones. For we cannot love Jesus without experiencing love for our brother. This warm overflowing love will flow out to everyone when deep sorrow for our cold indifferent heart—which prevented us from upholding the weak, difficult ones—takes place in us and causes us to change. This happens only when our eyes are opened to the standard of God's Word.

We must repent that we no longer take God's Word seriously, that we dare to set up our own standard of behaviour and are satisfied when we fulfill it. We are like the Pharisees: we—perhaps very enthusiastically— participate in the pious life. We pray, we go to church and Bible class, we tithe more or less, we have separated ourselves from the world, we do not do this or that any more. This is to say, we measure ourselves with our own yardstick. But God will measure us according to His standard, and He has shown it to us very clearly in His Word. So we will have no excuse when we come into judgment.

Therefore, the reason for our lack of repentance—for us personally as well as for the churches and Christian communities—is that we do not accept God's standard, His word for our life. We do not feel obliged to obey His command, "Give, and it will be given to you; good measure pressed down, shaken together, running over"

(Luke 6:38). Or "go the second mile" (Matthew 5:14). No, we protect ourselves on our pious journey by clinging to certain ways that make us feel we are better than worldly people. We go on putting aside as much as possible for ourselves instead of giving to those in distress or for the preaching of God's Word.

We disregard God's Word or interpret it to suit ourselves in our uncleansed lives. We do what we like in our relationship with our fellow men, with our money, in everything. We do not measure ourselves by the Scripture so are not upset by the things we do or say: our prayer life, our relationship to our fellow men, our loose mouths that say so much that is destructive in judging others. In all these we are not controlled by the law of love.

We must repent for having so little repentance! We must repent because the Pharisaical spirit is living in us—John the Baptist said to men, "Who warned you to flee from the wrath to come"?—and we actually believe that we can escape the wrath because we believe in Jesus Christ. The Pharisees said, "We have Abraham as our Father." We say, "Our church or our Christian community is our mother. We live by grace so will escape the coming wrath." We must repent of such thoughts and words for they bring God's judgment. It was this attitude that caused John the Baptist to say to the Pharisees, "You brood of vipers," then, "bear fruit that benefits repentance" (Matthew 3:7, 8).

Fruit of change, conversion, change of mind—that is what God is waiting for—otherwise the axe will be laid to our root, because "every tree that does not bear good fruit is cut down and thrown into the fire". Whose life shows forth much of the fruit of the Spirit: "love, joy, peace, patience," that the Scripture talks about? (Galatians 5:22). Is the light of joy shining on our face? Does our life and disposition testify to peace instead of quarreling and

48

fighting? These are listed among the fruits of the flesh, 'enmity, strife, jealousy", that are under God's judgment (Galatians 5:20). Who can testify to the fruit of patience even during the distress of illness or with difficult people? Who can claim the fruit of kindness that sees only the good in others? Who has love that covers a multitude of sins instead of talking about them, exposing them? Who can witness to the fruit of gentleness, a humble, gentle spirit that does not blow up in anger? Who can say he is always friendly?

The Apostle Paul writes in his letter to the Galatians (5:23) that against the fruit of the spirit there is no law. But God prefers His charge where the fruits are lacking as we can see with the fruits of the flesh: "those who do such things shall not inherit the Kingdom of God." That is not said to the church of the Old Testament but to the church of the New Testament which believes in Jesus Christ. What good is faith when it does not bear fruit?

The right standard of measurement is found in God's Word. When we accept His measurement, the command "repent" must be His most important one to us. It must be fundamental to our very way of life.

Chapter 7

God the Father Is Waiting for the Love of His Children, Their Homecoming through Repentance

Repent! Not only for disobeying God's commandments in the Sermon on the Mount, but especially for our chief sin—the sin against God Himself, which the Scripture tells us always brought the greatest punishment—the breaking of the first commandment which demands that we love Him above all else. How we grieve God's heart because we do not love Him, because we ignore Him or love Him half-heartedly.

God is a Father who is love, who plans every lovely thing for the children of men: the sunshine, the bird's song, the trees, the fields and flowers, the mountains and lakes, the beauty of the earth and sky. He waits like every earthly father to see if His children find pleasure in what He has done for them, if they thank Him, and if their love for Him grows greater. But our Heavenly Father, who created us and loves us with unspeakable love, waits in vain. From whom does He receive thanks and praise for all His grace? The birds sing their songs of praise, the flowers bloom to His glory, but we His children, who are also His creation, remain silent. Even those who have had the spiritual rebirth give little praise to Him. If we enjoyed His creation would not our love for Him be kindled? If we thanked God for all His favours great and small—the roof over our heads, our daily bread, or because the Father again and again provides joy upon joy for His children—would not our faces shine?

But in what home—especially among Christians—does one hear songs of praise to the Father, glorifying Him out of a joyful, grateful, loving heart? Yes, repent! Turn from your ungratefulness. Repent because we grieve the Father's heart and bring Him suffering instead of joy. He says in His Word: "I am weary of bearing" (Isaiah 1:14) and "You have burdened me with your iniquities' (Isaiah 43:24).

Who among His people lives wholeheartedly with the desire to bring joy to His heart; and because of love for Him wishes to thank Him continuously for all His grace?

Yes, let us repent of our ingratitude! It is a disgrace the way we accept God's blessings as though they were our due, and disregard the Giver's heart—who planned them all in love for us—by not giving Him the love and thanks He so desires.

Oh, how often we are hard as rocks. How often we sadden Him who has loved us more than anyone has ever loved us, who has sacrificed more than anyone has ever sacrificed, who gave His best for us, suffering excruciating torture and death—because we do not love Him or thank Him.

We are ashamed when we have been ungrateful to our earthly parents who dearly loved us and sacrificed so much for us. We are sorry when we sadden them and hurt their loving hearts. Shouldn't we be ashamed and brokenhearted because we have been so ungrateful to our Heavenly Father, and saddened Him by not responding to His sacrificial love with our love and thankfulness? When He punishes us as an earthly father would, we rebel against him instead of responding with loving confidence. This saddens Him, too, because we are His children.

It is as though everything in nature, the stones, the rocks and mountains echoes from this call: repent, take stock of yourself! Realize what you have done to your God! Change your ways all you who are indifferent towards God who is love, all you who do not love Him wholeheartedly, who do not trust Him. Yes, repent, and the Kingdom of Heaven will be "at hand" where God, who is the centre of the Kingdom, is loved. The Kingdom of Heaven will be "at hand" on earth wherever the children of men repent and turn from sinning against God, who is love—turn and begin to love Him, trusting Him, surrendering their wills to Him in everything.

Jesus shouts the word "repent" because He yearns for us and for our love, because He longs for us to incline our hearts towards Him. Yes, He calls: turn from the way you love the world, the way you love other human beings and yourselves. Change your way from now on to love Me and the Father. Then We will come to you and abide with you, and Heaven will be "at hand".

The repentance-call is God's salvation-call, for turning around means coming home to God. The degree of homecoming we experience depends on the degree of repentance we have; for it is repentance that brings us into closer union and communion with God, inclining more of Heaven to our life.

Is there anything more joyful here on earth than the grace of contrition and repentance? Can we reach for anything greater than this grace?

When Jesus began His gospel message with the word "repent", the love offer of His salvation, His wooing of us, was inherent within it. But also within it was God's grief over His children who had turned away from Him. He now must call them home, so He shouts: "Turn around, change, be converted back to God!" For His children are far away from Him. They no longer have the close relationship that children have who stand in love and confidence towards their Father. They have become strangers to Him. Does not a father long for His children? Does He not want them to come home to Him? A father without children is not a father. A father whose children have left him to go to foreign lands is full of sorrow. As truly as Jesus wept over Jerusalem—because He wanted to gather His children as a hen gathers her chickens—the Father's heart weeps today. For God is one God, the Trinity, who is the same yesterday, today and forever; and He grieves over His children who have been called but do not come.

We should repent in whatever area of our lives we do not come to God, wherever we are too wrapped up in earthly creatures, our professions, or the material things of this world. It has grieved His father-heart because He waits for us in vain. When He has tried to call us home through punishment we have responded with apathy. We have not returned home to Him. What else shall He do with us? When we do not answer His call to repentance in Revelation 2 and 3—where all the promises of the Gospel come to their culmination at the end of the age—God's just wrath will come upon us for there is no other way to call men home.

Oh, how difficult mankind makes it for their Creator God and Father! His church especially makes it hard for Him—though they should know their Father more intimately through the Lord Jesus Christ—by not turning from their selfish ways as they witness the signs of the end-time. Many still are striving for their own honour, still advancing their own cause while claiming to be fighting for the cause of God's Kingdom. They are maintaining their own positions while pretending to strive for the truth. How blind are they who call themselves His children, who still keep their idols, who are not convicted of their greatest sin: that they deprive Him of their love.

How long must the Father call "repent" because His

53

children cause such suffering to His Father-heart? He waits for one thing only—the repentance of His children. Let us "today, when we hear His voice" harden not our hearts.

Chapter 8

Repentance, the Commandment of the Hour, the Call of the End-time

"Repent" was the call of John the Baptist who prepared the way for Jesus. He made known but one way that we could receive Jesus, the way of repentance. As it is written: "Prepare the way of the Lord, make His paths straight, . . . and the rough ways shall be made smooth" (Luke 3:45). Only when repentance has prepared the way—the rough places made smooth, the rocks removed—can the Lord the King come, because He then finds a pathway on which He can come to the children of men. John the Baptist shows us that Jesus' coming requires men who prepare the way by standing in repentance. It was that way when Jesus came the first time, and it will be that way again when He comes the second time. The Scripture tells us this in many ways. It says that before Jesus' coming, at the end-time, Elijah will again appear as a preacher of repentance (Malachi 4:5). Also in the end-time the repentance call will be heralded throughout the world by the two witnesses (Revelation 11:3–6).

Repentance, as well as judgment, has to start in God's church. At the end-time, Israel will undergo a tremendous repentance which will be brought on by grief at the Messiah's appearing, when they recognize the one they crucified. But how shall the Jews come to repentance when the church has not led the way? To whom shall Jesus come as returning Bridegroom, and whom shall He take to Himself, if not the ones who are standing in repentance? Did He not first come to John the Baptist's disciples who were in the repentance movement? (John 1:35–42). They were the first ones to be called as His disciples. He will not do it differently at His return. Therefore, in our time the responsibility is much greater for the individual believer, for a church, to repent. For we are living in the atomic age, the beginning of the end-time, the time of the fulfilment of the prophecy for Israel. The Scripture has promised for the end-time, when the fig tree begins to turn green, that the Jews will return to the country of their fathers. God is now waiting, the whole world is waiting, for His own to repent, to prepare the way so the Lord can come to redeem His church and take it to Himself. Then the long awaiting of all creation will come to an end because the redeemed have returned to Zion and Jesus' church has come to its fulfilment.

Yes, all mankind, the entire world is waiting for those who will repent. What other call should be the command of the hour for this terrible age that is in the shadow of atomic war—since the weapon of destruction has already been discovered—than this one, "Repent!"? The atomic age has one thing to say to us: the most terrible judgments are forthcoming. Do not these wars that threaten us have the appearance of the trumpet judgments in Revelation 8? This chapter describes the terrible devastation that will take place, how a third of mankind will be killed through such a war. When this was read in past centuries it was impossible to imagine such a thing. Now, even a child knows it is possible. Yes, it has already begun, for atomic tests are already destroying nature.

Never before has judgment of the world been so imminent. In former judgments it was always God's concern that the people would repent. We know now—when the most terrible judgments are imminent—that His concern for this is greater than ever before. Yes, today it is very great since it concerns the final preparation for the Lord's return. We see it in the book of Revelation in the end-time when one stroke of judgment after another falls upon the earth in the trumpet judgments and in the bowls of wrath. God's question is always present: will they repent? But how often it is said, "and they still did not repent" (Revelation 2:21; 9:20, 21; 16:9, 11).

Oh, that this would not be said of us! Now, when God's judgment reaches the culmination point, the time has come for the repentance movement in the churches. How else can God's church be saved from wrath? Who shall escape His wrath? Truly, Holy Scripture has but one message: who are they who will escape God's wrath? Its answer is—only those who have broken hearts, those who repent. Jesus wants His own to escape the wrath. The Scripture tells us that His people are not supposed to go through the terrible time of the anti-Christ. Jesus speaks about an escape from the terrible things that will happen. In Luke 21:36 He calls us to watch "that you may have strength to escape all these things that will take place and to stand before the Son of Man."

Yes, we must wake up and repent, we must change so we can escape these terrible judgments. How can it come about? When we allow ourselves to be judged every day in our personal lives and in our churches. Only the one who surrenders himself to judgment—who loves Jesus as his Judge and gives Him full sway to judge in his life—will be able to receive Jesus as the returning Bride-groom (II Thessalonians 1:7–10). We read about men who did not look upon Jesus as Judge. He appears to them with His tremendous wrath and they cry out for the mountains and hills to fall on them to cover them and protect them against the wrath of the Lamb (Revelation 6:16).

End-time is judgment time. We are now entering into this end-time so now is the final hour for re-

57

pentance—that we may be judged here and now and so escape the later judgment. That will be the grace of the rapture; for rapture means to be raptured out of this world that is now ripe for judgment and to be drawn up to the Lord (I Thessalonians 4:16–18). The entire church will not participate in it. The Scripture states clearly that "without sanctification no one will see the Lord". When Jesus appears—revealed as the Holy One in all His majesty and glory—no one can come directly before His face or by His side unless he has been sanctified, transformed into His image. This comes about only through His chastening—when we allow Him to judge us.

For this reason and because it is the last hour, the trumpet call is heard from Heaven, "Repent". Who of us receives this call? Who of us proclaims it? It is important for the whole church to be called to repentance, for whole countries to repent, for repentance to come forth in all the world so God can stop His judgments. God is not looking for repentance in us for just our own sake— that we as individuals escape the terrible time that shall come—but for the sake of our world, for all of mankind that is blindly walking towards horrible destruction. Do we sense at this time—when God's grace is ending, when His patience is passing and His wrath is ready to pour out upon the world—how horrible the judgments will be? Our repentance must be in proportion to our sins. A great grieving and weeping should start amongst us.

It is we, the church of God, who have accumulated throughout history God's judgment for our lack of repentance. Oh, that we would not continue it in this end-time! The Pharisees and many of the pious ones were among those at Jesus' first coming who did not want their security disturbed. They said, why does John the Baptist continually insist on this one thing: repentance, repentance! It is the same today. When one points the finger again and again at this one thing, many people think it is a fanatical, one-sided, sad Christianity; that it is not the Gospel. But it is Biblical. It is the Gospel. Contrition and repentance bring forgiveness for our sins and bring us joy. It is the only way that Jesus comes to us and saves us from judgment. For that reason it is the call of this hour. What grace will be given to the one who stands in repentance in this end-time! The repentant will receive as much grace as others will receive the judgment that will fall upon the world. Then Jesus in magnificent glory coming in the clouds of Heaven will take the repentant to Himself. Yes, in a moment of time he will be changed. The more humble he was in repentance, the higher he will be lifted up. The more he was wearing the garment of repentance, weeping over his sins, the more he will be clothed with the wedding garment shining like the sun (Matthew 13:43). Then will he enter the wedding chamber.

Yes, unrepentance and judgment correspond. But repentance, redemption, and glorification, which is beyond our imagination, correspond too. Therefore, the call to repentance is God speaking for the end-time about which His Word says; "Blessed are those who hear and who keep what is written therein!" (Revelation 1:3; 22:7). Blessed are those who respond to the call of God's love-offering for they already experience something of the Kingdom of Heaven, and are prepared to celebrate with Him the wedding of the Lamb. "He who testifies to these things says, 'Surely, I am coming soon.' Amen. Come, Lord Jesus!"

PRAYER FOR REPENTANCE

Dear Lord Jesus, I ask Thee for what I long to have in my life: Thy greatest gift of grace, repentance.

Send me by Thy grace the Spirit of truth that I may recognize myself in Thy light and see the depth of my sin. Help me through Thy Word that it may convict me as Thy standard for my thinking and speaking, for my ways and doing, for my work and actions. Keep me from applying my own cheap standards. Bind me to the measurement of the Sermon on the Mount that I may see myself as Thou dost see me, that I may judge myself as Thou wouldst judge me if I had not repented of my sin.

Give me through Thy Holy Spirit sensitivity to recognize in everything that happens to me especially in Thy chastening—Thy loving admonition to repentance, and that I may respond to it willingly.

Answer my prayer by giving me a broken heart, not one that is self-righteous and self-satisfied, but one that is always able to weep anew over its sins and is then able to rejoice for Thy forgiveness.

I thank Thee that Thou wilt surely answer this prayer, because Thou dost enjoy more than anything else a sinner who repents. Therefore, Thou dost require tears of repentance from us. I do not want to look on my hard impenitent heart but upon Thee, my Lord Jesus Christ, who came to destroy all self-righteousness and hardness of heart, and who has won for us by His redemption a new heart that is soft and humble.

Make me continue in the prayer of faith until my hard heart has melted, and I am able to weep over the things I have done to God and to my fellow men. Give me the grace to weep over my old nature, over my hardness, lack of mercy and kindness, my evil speaking about others, my jealousy and envy, my insincerity, my dependence on human beings and the material things of this world. Bring about a complete change in me.

I thank Thee, Oh Lord, that Thou art calling for what I still do not have, repentance, and that by its coming my love for Thee will grow out of it. Let me this way—through the redeemed and happy life of a pardoned sinner—praise Thee here on earth and be prepared for Thy return, so that I might enter with Thee in glory to the Marriage of the Lamb. Amen.